The
PERISHING

The
PERISHING

Sherod Santos

W. W. NORTON & COMPANY

New York • London

For information about permission to reproduce selections from this
book, write to Permissions, W. W. Norton & Company, Inc.,
500 Fifth Avenue, New York, NY 10110

The text of this book is composed in Perpetua with the display set in
Caslon Open
Composition by R. Tedoff
Manufacturing by The Courier Companies, Inc.
Book design by Julia Druskin
Production manager: Andrew Marasia

Library of Congress Cataloging-in-Publication Data
Santos, Sherod, 1948–
    The perishing / by Sherod Santos.—1st ed.
        p. cm.
    ISBN 0-393-05166-8 (hardcover)
    I. Title
    PS3569.A57 P47 2003
    811'.54—dc21   2002003424

W. W. Norton & Company, Inc., 500 Fifth Avenue, New York N.Y. 10110
www.wwnorton.com
W. W. Norton & Company Ltd., Castle House, 75/76 Wells Street, London
W1T 3QT

1 2 3 4 5 6 7 8 9 0

for Lynne

Still glides the Stream, and shall for ever glide;
The Form remains, the Function never dies.

Contents

III.

IV.

V.

VI.

Acknowledgments

Grateful acknowledgment is made to the editors of the following journals, in which these poems first appeared:

Connecticut Review: "A Dervish for Ferdinand de Saussure," "Hill Road in Ukiah"
HEart: "Greencastle"
The Kenyon Review: "Book of Blessings," "Carousel," "A Moment," "The Monument," "A Valley in the Shadow of North Hollywood"
Literary Imagination: "Café Society," "A Sound Like Rain"
Margie: The American Journal of Poetry: "Landscape with Missing Figure"
The Nation: "A Baker's Dozen for Zachary" (as "Riddle"), "Hymn to Necessity"
The New Yorker: "Dairy Cows at Crawford Farm" (as "Dairy Cows of Maria Cristina Cortez")

Quarterly West: "Triptych" (as "The Island")

Raritan: "The Art of the Landscape," "The Perishing"

Slate: "After Catullus," "The Fostering," "Llandudno," "Illuminated Manuscript," "Romeo & Juliet," "Small Variations"

Smartish Pace: "Stranger at the Ashwood Threshold," "Summer Solstice, Islandmagee"

TriQuarterly: "Berlin," "Driftwood"

The Virginia Quarterly Review: "Red Advancing" (as "Love & Neglect")

Yale Review: "The Talking Cure," "Smoke Tree"

"Book of Blessings," "Dairy Cows at Crawford Farm," "Illuminated Manuscript," "Stranger at the Ashwood Threshold," and "A Valley in the Shadow of North Hollywood" were reprinted in *The Breath of Parted Lips: Voices from the Robert Frost Place*, CavanKerry Press, 2000. "Book of Blessings," "Illuminated Manuscript," "Romeo & Juliet," and "The Talking Cure" were reprinted in *Poets of the New Century*, David R. Godine, 2001.

I would also like to thank the University of Missouri–Columbia for both its advocacy and support of the literary arts, and for providing such a welcoming space to so many young poets and writers.

The epigraph to the collection is from section VIII of St.-John Perse's *Anabasis*; the epigraph to "The Talking Cure" is from Canto V of Dante's *Inferno* (author's translation).

Un grand principe de violence commandait à nos moeurs.

—St.-John Perse

THE PERISHING

It began as a sound in the nettle trees
that grew along the runoff ditches near the lake,
the whisper of a dry wind rattling the leaves,
the unsettling air adrift with ash.
                                    It began
as a sound, though hushed and small,
that in no time at all became a constant
and upwelling thing, the soft chorale
of something unsayable slipping away,
thinning out like an inwardness
over the mineral waste, or like a memory lost
in the evanescence of remembering.
                                    Over
the burning lake it passed, this sound,
and even as the feelings it awakened in us
seemed gathered up into its passing,
tinged with the nothingness still to come,
it luffed and flared and coalesced
into shimmering planes of vanishing,
an immense, chimeric seepage
through some misweave in the weft of things,
for it was we eventually came to see
the sound
            of our own perishing,
the all-but-unthinkable erasure
that's both part of and apart from us,

a supersession so absolute,
so attuned to the particulars of our lives,
that even though it's there
in everything we've done, in every shadow
of the broadcast moon,
                              we barely think
to miss it now the time has come
to imagine ourselves all over again,
to imagine us as we'd been before
we heard that sound in the nettle trees
and recognized it for what it was.

I

ZERO AT THE BONE

Of nothing less, or more, or outside us,
Or within, of absolute forgetfulness,
Of all things most a life bereft, a plinth
Of air, a winter snow-fed sun that's sensed
Only in the figure of a passing thought,
Or the realization of what we thought
Of nothing for, that zeroing in
Of a self beguiled and, wanting n-
Othing, finds it wants it all the more.

A SOUND LIKE RAIN

Twice tonight I awakened to the soughing sound
Of rain and twice discovered it was only that,
Across the street, our recently widowed neighbor
Had left her garden sprinkler on, its standing water
Here and there welling up over the concrete curb
In loose, collected rivulets of wet, a moon-lit runoff
Less like spilled water than the dispossessing ghost
Of water sluicing down the gutters and away.

LLANDUDNO

Rigged with a sea-shawl of twilight and mist,
The refurbished eighteenth-century boardwalk
Emptied of its visitors, the souvenir stands shut down,
And like the *corwg* housed in a local museum
We toured that day, its broad-planked floor strained
Against the anchor of its history. But no telling

What prospect the mind beheld, or the body
Remembered, to find itself wrong-footed and alive
To four or five skinheads stepping from a stairwell
In the parking lot, their forearms barred with swastikas,
And embedded in the leather of their combat boots,
A crosshatch metalwork of razor blades.

THE FOSTERING

A twilight like quicksilver spilled out
On the Sound resembles more old pewter
Near the end, and the conversation
Following darkens by degrees, giving up

Its feints of sparkle to the evening's alcohol.
Children of time, my brother and I
Remember how, in the summer
Of his sixteenth year, my fourteenth

That September, our mother moved back
Into the house she'd only three months earlier
Labored through one long afternoon
To empty of its belongings, of everything,

That is, except for a black-and-white TV set,
Two mattresses, and a rosewood Belvedere
Armoire she had found so loveless she'd left
It out one winter as a feeder for the birds.

And just as she had left that day, she reappeared,
Summoned back through the twilight by
A conjurer's wand, our father away
On a business trip, the moving van in tow.

In a day-and-a-half, the willowware uncrated,
The paintings rehung at the same
Nail holes, she sat down finally on the couch
And waited, and readied herself, steadied

Her nerves with a sigh she never quite
Let go . . . For what? For nothing less
Than a miracle, some self-displacing sleight
Of hand whereby we'd all take up again

The life that she'd abandoned. I leaned
Close to her and started to ask, but then
Said (senselessly), "You look sad." Well past
My understanding, she smiled at me,

Switched on and off an unplugged lamp,
Then setting her gaze on a dream
Deferred to the swirling fan-blades overhead,
She began aloud to imagine herself,

To imagine us, too, in a future we soon
Realized was as inescapable as it was
Unreal. . . .
                A cough. A glass refilled.
Outside, the watery dark has risen

Like a sea, a sea in which the mind unbuoyed
Descends in slurring channels through
A silted deep no memory stirs.
But in the dark inside, that moment flares,

A brimming waterdrop, lucent, formless,
Heavy with the failure still to come,
And then, like a star, it slides
Down the blue ether pane of her face.

HILL ROAD IN UKIAH

Even as I recall the dream I remember it as real:
Cheri and Bruz racing across the uncut grass
To meet her old black Packard reconfigured
As a hearse; and she is as she always was,

A stalwart country woman in a cotton frock,
So unafraid of dying she's content, it seems,
To drive herself, unescorted, up through
The slanting shadows of the hillside graves.

for M.V.S. (1903–1994)

GREENCASTLE

Why complicate what is simple? The prison lights
Across Lough Foyle, sea stones drying in a tin pan
On the windowsill, and on the fold-out cot,
Ben asleep, his radio headphones still turned on.

SMALL VARIATIONS

In the Hospice gardens, midday in the bright sun,
A woman of thirty or thirty-five, too weak,
Exhausted, or disinclined to walk the few yards back
To her room, raises her pale blue hospital gown
And in one slow motion squats along the pathway to pee.
And standing there beside her, her hopelessly
Embarrassed father, unable to look, unable not to look.

❖

The lamp turned off, the curtains white in folds.
First an ear, an eyebrow, the curve of her shoulder,
The small scallop of her collarbone, and gradually
His dead wife appears to him, just as she'd done
Thirty years before when he'd take the night train
Home from the Clinic, thinking his way through
The sequence of kisses he'd give her on his return.

❖

For days on end she sits beside her sleeping son,
Her fingers busy stitching and unstitching a large
Needlepoint picture of a lane down which red-
Jacketed men on horseback ride. But how to explain
The shame that now comes over her? The shame
That she's already begun (even as he lies dying)
To imagine a world in which she couldn't imagine him.

CAROUSEL

He'd just switched off the overhead light and stretched out
Full-length on the sofa. An open window. A shade

Between the rose and ochres of a long twilight in mid-
September swamped the outlying, mottling sands

Freaked with patches of pampas grass. Not a breath of wind,
Not a sound anywhere for the time he took

To take his shower and lie down for a nap before dinner.
It's odd how he recalls it all so clearly still,

That guttering hour in summer fifteen years ago,
The quiet end of a travel day: a plastic cup of orange peels,

An empty half-bottle of some sweet wine he'd found
In the hotel mini-bar. And he remembers, too, a car horn

Sounding in the street below, then laughter and voices
Spilling out from the lobby into a parking lot beyond.

And then a fight broke out. He must've fallen asleep
By then, for the garbled stream of insults seemed

Channeled through the margins of his consciousness:
Two men, he imagined, around whom

Others formed the cordon of a makeshift ring
Where, like two lunging animals galled

By a closing swarm of bees, the crackle
Of threats and goadings rose to prick them on,

The violence of it spurred, retributive, tribal somehow,
Somehow opening outward into waves

Of malice and aggression. It was as if
Some great perturbation in the human heart

Had by an unchecked excess loosed
Its mindless riot on the evening air, and the air in turn

Now bristled with a staticky spasm of its own.
Throughout it all he'd barely moved,

Had scarcely known what he could do, but then
He feared that they might actually kill each other.

He called the front desk and they said they'd go,
But for what still seems the longest time,

An eternity of groans followed by the heavy thud
Of blows, it did not stop. And then it did.

And then there was a sound like hose-water
Splashing off asphalt, a car door closing, and tinged

With a salt impression of the sea, a shelving breeze
Rose ushering in what it took him a moment

To recognize as the hollowed-out, fricative, wound-
Down notes of the deserted boardwalk carousel.

II

THE MONUMENT

Ten times Tamerlane's fabled wall of blood and severed limbs,
And even where they did not exist, even where they
    had never existed,
We'd have had to kill them anyway, we'd have had to kill them all.

For in 1915 the Young Turks counting heads conceived an epoch-
Making joke: How many Armenians does it take to build a wall
Ten times that which Tamerlane built from the body parts of men?

But the answer was monumental, the answer was something
Heretofore unimaginable on such grand scale, the answer,
They knew, was modern: Eventually they'd have to kill them all.

Decades later, having counted up the Jews, Hitler begins to brood,
"For who," he asks his cabinet, "remembers the Armenians
    anymore?"
And even if they did not exist, even if they had never existed,

The Gypsies and homosexuals, the Freemasons, J.W.s,
    dabblers in art
When added to that already numberless sum might easily make
A shadow of Tamerlane's storied wall of blood and severed limbs;

So next he figures the Christians in, and those who might be
    faint of heart,
The listless, the stutterers, the bookish, and halt, and he figures how
(With the help of a roach poison, Zyklon B) he might actually
    kill them all.

And so the wall continued to rise, and so the wall, as if framed
And lighted in a photo by Leni Riefenstahl, inflated into history,
Even though history did not exist, even though it has never
    existed.

In the Soviet Union the bourgeoisie is Lenin's self-appointed task,
And when Stalin takes over the job's been done with greater skill
Than Tamerlane dreamed could raise a wall from the body parts
    of men;

Nevertheless, Stalin will go on tracking them down, in the parks
    and cafés,
Among sporting groups and writers' guilds, factory heads and Party
Leaders, he will go on killing them, too, eventually he will
    kill them all,

Until the wall makes a relic of the Führer's dream, for it's a wall
Composed (just imagine it!) from the corpus of one's
    own citizens,
Even though citizens did not exist, even though they
    had never existed.

So when Mao makes war on the landlords and intellectuals,
    the pacifists
And sly imperialist spies, when even where they do not exist
He mortars them into his own Great Wall of blood
    and severed limbs,

He conceives of it as possible, so unnumbering are his kind,
To refigure a wall that's all on earth still visible from the moon,
· If only he can go on killing them, if only he can kill them all.

And ever higher it grows, well beyond the reach of thought itself,
Until hunkered in the jungle one afternoon a man named Pol Pot
Speculates how, even if they do not exist, even if they
     have never existed,

He could eliminate all who ever wore glasses, or brewed
     sweet tea,
Or whistled a tune, the zeroes spiraling off his pen like the cries
Of the dead, the *O O O*'s that no one not even God can hear,
For as Tamerlane in his providence knew, the wall is the wall
Of oblivion, and even if it did not exist, even if it
     had never existed,
We'd have had to kill them anyway, we'd have had to kill them all.

CAFÉ SOCIETY

Scarfed in a thin umbrellaed shade more rose
Than golden now the sun has slipped
The steepled sundial of St. Séverin,
The ousted small-time military ruler,
Exiled in Paris since 1984,
Now takes his morning coffee at the street-side
Tables of Les Deux Magots, a habit he wouldn't
Have imagined safe even two or three years
Before. But like that cool, affluent stream
Of stylish people who surround him there,
Politics has its passing fashions, and often
These mornings leave him discomposed
To think that no one anymore wants him dead.

And so, in time, he finds he's less inclined
To leave the narrowing shade of his table,
A fact not lost on the salmon-vested staff
He commands by tips doled out deliberately
With an air of moneyed complacence;
And so, in time, he has managed by
A simple nod of the head, or a finger raised
To encircle the thin-glazed rim of his cup,
To alert them to the privilege of such
Services as he now requires. But nothing
In history is ever lost, and something about
That mute exchange stirs like a spoon

The memory of an incident a human-rights
Group once pointed up in a U.N. document
Years before.
                    One evening, for the benefit
Of three mothers who'd been summoned
To watch through the open window
Of a barber shop, a badly beaten
Milicias youth was carried inside, stripped
Of his clothes, and bound spread-eagle
To a tabletop. They'd thought, at first,
He might be the one-armed riverman's son,
The one who trapped chameleons
He'd then sell for coins in the village square.
But finally they couldn't say for sure,
For the battered body laid out that way
Had seemed, somehow, unreal to them,
The bound limbs merely symbolical,
The bruised torso illumined like
An altarpiece, or a Christmas crèche,
By the light of a hand-held kerosene lamp
Around which insects thronged and fell
In a flurry of gilt enamelings.
And in that weird, unworldly glow,
The commanding officer conveyed
By a simple nod of the head, a finger raised
To trace an imaginary ring in the air,
When the shocks should be administered
From a jumper cable attached at one end
To a dry cell battery in a transport truck,

At the other end to the grotesquely swelling
Spectacle of the rebel soldier's genitals.

Of course, all of that happened years ago.
Its time has passed. And now the idle days,
So many he's given up keeping track, stack up
Like saucers on a tabletop. And it's from
Their spent endowment that he pushes back,
Lights his first cigarette of the morning,
And makes his way unhampered through
That lustral wash of people on the boulevard
St. Germain des Pres, a liquid element
Which has come to be, in its haute bourgeois
Anonymity, an otherness he enters as easily
As the past now passes out of memory.

THE ART OF THE LANDSCAPE

for Mark Strand

In Sebastião Salgado's photographs
Of Rwandan refugees in Tanzania,
A viewer gets lost momentarily in the epic,
Bosch-like register of death and human suffering,
The far-flung encampments of washpots,
Lean-tos, scattered rags, the emaciated, fly-
Ridden children, the scabbed, hollow-eyed
Men and women gathering twigs, or skewering
Rats for a cook-fire, a populace that appears
To have wandered here across the salt expanse
Of a drought-stricken, uninhabitable earth.
And their suffering is not made less of
Than their suffering is, nor their stares
Made more consolable than we've come
To expect from a grief beyond the reach
Of mercy, for everything about them,
We realize, will go on forever and always.

And yet somehow in the face of this same
Unspeakable harm, a photographic fact
Distills the air with a gilt precipitate
Apportioned it by a sunrise that has opened up
A thin empyrean of golden light, the strata
Of cloud illumined with some vaulted
Aspect of sublimity such as one might see

In a nineteenth-century landscape painted
By Kensett or Whitteredge or Heade,
Though the light of those paintings, infused
With an aureate splendor borne of plenitude
And awe, outshines a world composed
In shades of everything except what's human.
And isn't that, after all, what worries us most
About this picture? A beauty unchastened
By experience? The idea that with deliberate care,
With weighed precision, the photographer
Has taken the measure of some pale
Effulgence that falls with what is hardly grace
On the whole anonymous tragedy held
In the hollow of an outstretched hand?
Or is it more that this is a landscape
From which human suffering is not dispelled?
That theirs is a misery before which
The beautiful, however haphazard,
However unwilled, might insusceptibly
Make itself known? That contrary to some line
We've drawn between what we honor
And what deplore, the two might actually
Subsist somewhere within the province
Of each other's worlds?

A rent in memory,
And *Time* recalls another photograph
By a photojournalist free-lancing shots
Out around the benchlands near Kosovo.
In a small, poppy-filled clearing in the woods

Two hundred meters above the mountain
Village of Velika Krusa, he has stumbled on
A Serbian soldier who, except for certain
Small details, seems poised above the history
He's making, afloat in the ether of a storybook
World where even our fears are transfigured.
For within that world the soldier is tensed
And bent to play an English rosewood upright
Piano whose burnished surface is haloed
In the tailings of a winter sun. To the right
Of him, there is stacked up what appears to be
A cache of musical instruments; to the left,
A mounded tarpaulin against which rests
A Russian Dragunov sniper's rifle
With a nightscope and box magazine.
There couldn't be more than an hour or so
Of daylight left. And were our visions
Keen enough, we could just make out,
Halfway up the mountainside, the access
To a shallow cave, and within that cave,
Hunkered together against the cold, what
Remains of a family of Albanian musicians
Whose upright piano that soldier plays.

The family—a grandmother and her brother,
A mother with her two daughters and son—
Has sheltered in the cave for eighteen days
On a week's supply of water and bread
And dried sausages. And so it happens

That beyond all sense, rising up through
The chill gradations of the mountain air,
The family hears, or imagines it hears,
The obscure but familiar chords of a Mozart
Concerto in D Minor; and so clearly
Does the music filter up off the valley floor
That they can tell from the luff of a single
Out-of-tune G flat key that their piano
Is the one being played, and that the person
Who plays it does so with exceptional
Tenderness and care. So much so that all
The while the music plays they find
Themselves inclining nearer the mouth
Of the cave, leaning out into the fleet andante
Of each carefully articulated measure.
And for what still seems a moment pitched
Well beyond the reach of space and time,
They take it all in, the thin, collecting overtones,
The loosely modulating lilts and falls,
The trills and tailed arpeggios, they take it all in
And hold it there, as if the weight of each note
Could quicken the mind's capacities,
As if the mind could actually abide such things
As a sniper's hands on the piano keys
Of a Mozart concerto in D Minor.

III

BERLIN

When my father broke his family's counsel
And re-upped for the airlift into Germany,
He stormed the black capital like Ecgtheow's son,
His tonnage downgraded to anthracite
From Amatol and TNT, such payloads
As custom still meted out to a city Grendeled
In the underworld of incendiary smoke.

BLACK CORSAGE (1880–1918)

Now that my idle life has reached its end
    Scooped out like a pearl from the mess I've been
Inclined to think unkindly is our age's church
    I can address you at last without offense
Without shrouding us both in circumstance
    And that flower you cautioned I never touch
I now wear on my sleeve like a black corsage
    Stinking of sickrooms camphor and rage

And since I dwell among those ineffable things
    Which you in your ignorance call nothings
I suppose nothing is what you'll make of this
    More's the pity for whenever you come
To weigh in your palm some vague impression
    Of the world beyond you'll remember it as
A continuo of what you'd feared most
    In the manuscripts Europe fed the host

Of choiring flames the fire-cure of oblivion
    That can never be doused or forgotten
Never be banked to silence no you must begin
    To accustom yourselves as I've done here
To this bracketed absence *(Guillaume Apollinaire)*
    To this ungloved handshake I hope extends
Beyond the one unkindness you won't forgive
    My undying my reader my sweet revenge

RED ADVANCING

Homage to Piet Mondrian

Out beyond the last grim hamlet's gaze,
He reflected on what reflected him,
A red cloud suggesting blood, later flame.

And later still the primary color of a mind
In thought, the thought itself advancing
Skyward through a space composed

In level planes of hardly human feeling.
It was, after all, a small matter of spirit,
An inner vision of the outer world,

And he considered it all routine enough,
The canon of proportions in a slant
Of light, the coloratura of the birdsong

That surrounded him as he smoked
And muttered on the towpath past
That state of nature he most deplored:

The nether land of God's color, green.
For what it's worth, he'd looked in all
The predictable places, the mise-en-scène

Of haycocked fields and watermills,
The gilt-limned trellis of a horizontal tree,
Even, for that matter, *l'esprit nouveau*

Of the Paris salon untouched as yet
By that quiet catastrophe called de Stijl.
But only in time would his self-styled

Civil servant soul concede this one
Coherent fact: the "poetic faculty" (or,
As he'd encountered it in Simonides,

"The word of things a picture is")
Was already there within him, rooted
Like a doubt which, blurred by years

Of indifference, now clarified
Into a smithy's anvil he'd one day
As a boy observed floating past

On the river Gein. As it happened,
He dismissed it all as a will-o'-the-wisp,
The shadow play of a blinking eye,

But then, years later, the mouth
Of the river debouched great heaps
Of burning glass—"sparks everywhere,"

The newspapers said, "and small waves
Polishing the driftwood fires"—
And suddenly it all came back to him,

The smithy's anvil, the light-crazed surface
Of the river Gein, and what it meant
To love a mystery like a work of art.

And remembering that made the boy
In him feel inexpressibly happy,
And the man in him turn dully away.

LANDSCAPE WITH MISSING FIGURE

As if scraped off first then scumbled over
With a spackled, metallic shade of gray,
The sea shone dull as lead that day, and the blue-
Chevroned geese were through calling across
The waterway, their raveled line
Falling like a rope behind the scattered dunes,
Or all at once angling upward like a water-
Spout into the salt-stirred air. Inked-in atop
A stone outcropping where the steep
Escarpment of the cliffs ascends a hundred feet
Above the bay, the seventy-eight-year-old
Thomas Hardy regards all this as context
For a man or woman, stooped by what
Appears to be a more than human burden,
Advancing alone along the wet pack
Left by the receding tide.
                              And so it is
That with ever-enlarging interest he observes
That figure's progress past the foreground
He's been laying out graphically in his head,
The fixed, unstable interplay of light
And shadow fired for only a brief half-hour
While the sun burns down to a grenadine stain,
A blood spot on the waterline. It is, you see,
His lifelong habit to worry an image
To the point that it will render up, limned

With the nacre of his thoughtfulness,
Some pearl-trace of its inner life. And likewise
He now asks himself what meaning
This possibly holds for him, this figure
Shawled in a ragged, sea-spun, soot-
Colored mist.
              It is, after all, the fall
Of 1919, and he has seen it all before,
The shell-shocked soldiers furloughed out
Along the loamy Weymouth lanes;
The pauper peasants harrowing twigs
Beside a burning heap of couch grass;
The destitute and broken, the incurable
And insane washed up like dreck
In the railyards, ditches, alleyways, and jails.
But this seems something different,
This seems something altogether strange,
And the more he tries to imagine it,
The more it seems this figure tends
From the asylum of his own memory.
But who, he wonders, would labor across
Such distances? The shade of that turf-
Faced Dorset boy, "The simple self that was,"
He'd banished to the stony pages of his prose?
The artfully unmasked genius manqué
Of Edwardian London's literary crowd?
Or was it, more likely, the shade of his poor
Mad Emma come to rail at him again
For the poverty he'd made of marriage,

For the belatedly heartfelt book of poems
He'd posthumously made of her?
Whatever it was, and from whatever
Inmost place it arose, it didn't take long
For the face to become, in the narrowing
Purpose of his mind's eye, an integral part
Of the landscape. And it didn't take long
Before everything there below him—
The breakwater, seawall, low-lying waves,
The pale dunes prinked with beach grass,
The cormorants roosted on the rocks
Offshore—before everything balanced
On the slender fulcrum of a world
Now poised between a nameless terror
On the one hand, an inexorable
Sorrow on the other.
                        Was this,
He wondered, the insight writing leads to
After all these years? The truth such endless
Shadings and relations leave to those
Who believe in them too faithfully
And too long? "Nevertheless,"
He reminds himself, "better to work
Than complain." So taking out a notebook
He carries in the pocket of his overcoat,
He begins to describe the multiple, thin,
Viridian bands the pier piles cast
On a stretch of sand, incidental enough,
As such things go, yet a part of the whole

All the same. He works that way intently
While the light still holds, and when
He looks up next the horizon's a smoldering
Ember gray, and that burdened figure out
Walking the shore has vanished altogether
As if carried away by the out-going tide.
Without the least thought of anyone (of this
He feels quite sure), the world is once again
Subsumed by the lapping shadow it becomes
At dusk. And it settles on him then
With a faint but clearly discernible pang
That travels slowly along his spine
To a widening space just behind the eyes,
It settles on him that he's now become
The "dead man walking" he'd foretold
Thirty years before, and that his days of happiness,
The days of happiness he has given others,
Will never amount to anything more
Than a random notation transcribed against
A life made up, in greater part, by plotting,
Rancor, book reviews, money, apostasy, and art.

AFTER CATULLUS

A penknife engraved first your name, then his,
Then a heart around them with a wedded plus,

Then an X across it all, the drawn out chronicle
Of your last uncontested crush still knuckling over,

Twenty years later, in the side yard of your parents'
House. For as I learned this evening, it was your

Crossed heart that broke, not his, and so turned
Romance into something fleshed, impregnable,

And almost shameless once those first taboos
Took a backseat to the round chord your plucked

Body struck: that overjoy you've rung so many times
By now you've grown unsure of what it was

You wanted then, before the dream had wearied
Of itself and sex stood through you like an ampersand.

And so, tonight, as you rise from your canopied
Childhood bed, I watch you watch those leafy

Shadows worry across the windowsill, and I feel
For a moment the presence of that lost thing

Out there in the lull of a late rain dying out,
In the moon transfusing through the windowpane,

And as if I'd tasted them myself, I feel for you
Those thousand kisses left upon the lips of other men.

STRANGER AT THE ASHWOOD
THRESHOLD

I.

Did he think that disguise would fool me? Gathering about
His balding head those filthy rags, poor-mouthing
His way beside my fire, then gazing into the looking glass
Of my bride's-mind to summon up the legend
I'd seen last at the ashwood threshold twenty years ago,
The husband who'd upped and sailed away on a black,
Oar-swept ship of war to a place he called . . . I call *Destroy*.

"Your son will vouch for me," he claimed, "I saw your king
On foreign soil. He wore a wine-dark, woolen cape
Fastened by a brooch inlaid with gold, a brooch on which
A great hound clenched and throttled to death a dappled fawn."
He knew, of course, I'd given Odysseus that very cape,
Had dyed its wool that royal red, had buckled its folds
With that same brooch. And so, I suppose, I passed his test.

The salt tears soaked my cheek. A fact he took in silently
Beneath his rags, though how could I not have recognized him
With his poet's words, his poet's unfazed self-concern
So skillfully playing my emotions? The truth is,
However much I loved that man in the wine-dark cape,
However much I'd longed for him, I'd have settled
For the man with thinning hair, the beggar-king of Ithaca.

II.

Having slept alone year after year in the upper story
Of our high-roofed home, having awakened nightly
In that rooted, rightly far-famed bed he'd built by hand
Around the bole of a thickset olive tree, I soon
Discovered there are two known gates through which
All dreams must come to pass. The first is made
Of ivory, cleanly carved, the second of polished horn;

Through ivory our dreams are will-o'-the-wisps, scant
Tracings on the air, through horn they're star-signs
We'd be wise to chart our futures by. It was through horn
It came that night he questioned me beside the fire,
The contest of twelve axes, one for each month
Of the year I'd lived through twenty times for him,
Housebound to the labor of my hardwood loom.

The thwarted suitors watched agog, he watched them watch,
Though no one saw (how could they?) how the hand
That strung his bow recalled my own hand spooling out
New wool, that drew on strength enough to strike
An arrow through a dozen axe-helve socket rings
Recalled the heart it took each night to climb back
Into the vaulted tomb of our empty, tree-housed bed.

III.

Waiting at the doorway while I was brushing back my hair,
Odysseus stood and stared across the unraked terrace
Gardens trashed from last night's welcome home.
One guttering pine-pitch torch still burned, its pool
Of light apotheosized to a ringing lyre—the singer's
Who had begged him calm his bloodlust, spare
One pauper soul among that heavy haul of slaughtered men.

He'd been every inch the hero then, spattered with gore,
His forehead glistening, dripping red. But this morning,
He looked to me just as he had looked before: his thin
Shirt clung like onion skin to his boxer's ropy
Shoulders, his young man's muscled chest and arms;
And as before, those faraway, slightly moonstruck eyes
Seemed focused on a flyspeck at the world's end.

It struck me then that, even as he stood there, steeped
In the memory of all this place brought home to him,
He labored at the anchor of whatever in me
Refused that death his heart most longed to master.
And as before, I could see it coming, his going away,
Those maddened gulls scavenging after the trim black ship
My harbored longings had driven out of reach.

IV

A BAKER'S DOZEN FOR ZACHARY

By all accounts miscounted, they are counted on by you,
As if words weren't meant to mean what they do,
As if their uprisings were a promise coming true
In the semblance of a riddle, in the name of one, too.

A DERVISH FOR FERDINAND DE SAUSSURE

Bored with homework, our eight-year-old
Has slipped out into the backyard where,
In a scribble of wide, unscripted twirls,
He rewrites the mind's resistance to
A language set on tracing how, in a world
Of signs, the word dislocates its significance,
Its sense represented in the sounds
It somehow cannot be (or for all intents
And purposes become), a dislocation
You'd think his light-headed body had
Inclined to when, spellbound by the logic
Of a recklessly upscaled, keening *eeeee*,
The world is whirled so roundly it up-
Ends the very ground he's walking on.

DAIRY COWS AT CRAWFORD FARM

County Antrim, Northern Ireland

Still road-weary but quite warmly stowed
Beneath a goose-down duvet in the B & B,
I awaken to a lowing stream of cows
Flooding the field behind a milking barn,

A scene that seems to have followed me here
From childhood, the traced illustrations
Of a nursery rhyme (their watercolors not even
Thought of once in over thirty-five years),

Or a Sunday's hour-long lesson on a notion
That surely eluded me then, *the peace
Which passeth understanding.* So framed,
The mind's rumination deepens like a dream,

And like a dream from which the mind's eye
Culls, not the particulars of a landscape
(Withheld, in any case, as sun and mist
Alike lift off the inwardly greening hills)

But the mute disbursements of a feeling
That's composed in part of earth and air,
So, too, my window kindles an impression
I can't separate from those dozen or more

Milk cows milling about the grasslands
Of the Crawford's farm. It follows then
That something within their cumbered
Motions through the morning air recalls

An instinct pastured where the slow, pacific
Form thought takes is given time to reflect
On thought: thought thinking thought,
And the once unthinkable end of thought,

Whereof one cannot speak, thereof one must
Be silent. So wherever they go, alone
Or at times beside themselves, wading
The mud lanes out from the dairy,

Or grazing the sketched-in grasses by a pond,
They move the way a slow-forming storm
Cloud moves, trolling the earth out of which
It draws, in the evanescence of a passing hour,

A heaviness it must soon become. And yet
A cow jumped over the moon, we're told,
And what has ever more easily slipped
The snare of its own burden, turned burden,

By nature, to beneficence, than the plush surprise
Releasing along their blood stream's course
A plenitude spiked, as Virgil noted,
With salt herb, lotus, and shrub trefoil.

A plenitude which, to temper that bitterness
We drink to warm and clarify the day,
I stream out into a steaming mug
Delivered, like gladness, on a breakfast tray.

DRIFTWOOD

Tumbled from the backwash of a fishing boat,
Laved in salt and damascened with worm-
Loops scrolling the long arm's length of it,
It rehearses in our son's musing hands
A history of fells and sail-roads, of flare-ups,
Strongholds, the terror-monger at last laid low,
And the gold-hoard hauled from its barrow.
Stripped from the tree of reckoning, arrayed
Against the world's unpunished harms,
May it still serve in the coming years to bolster
The peacemaker's heart in him, to steer him
Around whatever new perils must now
Precede that homecoming folktales tell us is
The end-all meaning of our journeying.

HYMN TO NECESSITY

With a chain saw and axe, I've spent a long
Morning cutting up a sycamore the storm
Brought down. For all ten years we've lived here,
It has shaded over our kitchen window, upheld
Various clothes lines, feeders, rope-plank swings,
The candle-lit rice paper Japanese lanterns,
And even, on one occasion, one corner
Of a straw-hooped canopy for a wedding.
So borne in mind, I've come to find that,
Rinsing dishes in the sink at lunch,
The space it's cleared over-brims itself
And turns what's not there outside in.
But how good the sun feels in its absence,
And how like absence to surprise me this way.

A VALLEY IN THE SHADOW OF NORTH HOLLYWOOD

As if cued to the first peach prayer-call of sunrise,
The scattered choir of radio alarm clocks
Summons the sleeping body to the mild surprise
Of a work-week morning in the suburbs;

Like clockwork, too, the born again wail
Of a garbage truck begins its broadcast mission
To release with each upended fall
The welling burden of our discontents.

Our first thoughts, then, are of garbage cans
And the human soul, that ancient service
By which the one laid low is taken in hand,
Impelled once more to reclaim its outcast

Station in the home; or, like the storybook fool,
Unheavened altogether on the paving stones,
A reminder that, no matter how fully
A soul comes clean, certain transgressions

Still reenact the passion play of divine neglect,
(A fate which by accepting we can overlook
When, for example, cresting the high prospect
Of an overpass, the sun relapses and the addict

Climbs back into the storm pipe he's made
His home). But look! Called back to that hour
Of reckoning, the pilgrim-trail of car lights slides
In slow succession down the valley floor,

And the underground sprinklers' sleeved,
Uplifted arms have left the lawns incensed,
The rinsed curbs blessed by waters to receive
Such pale illumination as one might see,

Or imagine one sees, when a garage door opens
And lo and behold it somehow happens
That a light both inside and out comes on
And for one brief moment turns everything gold.

BOOK OF BLESSINGS

The reserved and slightly weary-eyed doctor
In the ER who, having awakened him late,
Curled up in a blanket on the waiting room floor,
Said two times softly, "She'll be fine now,"
That doctor was writ in his Book of Blessings.

As were the windfall apples the horses ate
(Their trailing slobber's acrid stain
Like the wrack of nature across his hand)
At the Shaker village in Kentucky
Where his mother had gone to recover.

                                And the tears
Of his mother, muffled, exhausted,
Utterly undone by her night-long struggles
In the room next door, while the boy
Sat watching on a television screen
The man a following crowd called King,
Though the crowd surrounding did not bow down
In the Selma of 1965.

                    And yet
The King's high seeing still gazed beyond the fear
In everyone's eyes to a place made quiet
By him in them, so that the crowd in passing
Made a papery sound, like the scrape of leaves

(Or, as the boy now saw it, like the theme of leaves),
Across the threshold that opened within him there.

That, too, was writ in his Book of Blessings.

As were the songs he'd committed to memory,
The one about a fast-falling eventide,
The one about stardust and a garden wall;
And before that there was learning to read,
The alphabet, syllable, word, and phrase,
The vanishing point of the period,
The tripled period's placid sea . . .

                              And suspended
Roundly above that sea, the fluent figure
Of a risen moon, and the loosed imagining
Moon adds to speech, the sea change
Its four letters form in the mind of a boy
Sitting up in bed until the bed's no longer
A bed at all, but a boat whose filling spinnaker
Has hauled it out from a foreign shore
Overgrown with shadow-shapes and rustlings.

And his penis erect in a dream that boat
Now carries him toward, a dream in which
The towering secret of his begetting
Is at last spelled out in the bright pearl-droplets
Of a falling rain, as though the moon

Were weeping on the open sea,
And the sea were a body it yearned for.

                                    All that
Was writ in his book as well, all that
And more than he is able to recall tonight,
For after forty-eight years he has come to find
So many erasures appear there now,
So many passages torn out whole,

                            while in
The Book of Death the pages are already
Filling up, and in the Book of Silence,
And in the Book of Forgetting.

V

THE TALKING CURE

It exceeds all sorrows to tell you this,
To recount in the face of such misery
My little moment of remembered bliss.
                                                    —INFERNO

Eyes shut. Lapsed time. The 2 A.M. aquarium light.
The background noise of my parents' party
Winding down upstairs. A suspended moment
Between two worlds while the mind's uprooted
From a sleep that won't quite blink away,
And a woman from one or the other of those worlds
Who has found her way beside my bed saying,
Shhh, shhh, it's only me, though I can't imagine
Who *me* might be. And before I'm able to ask her,
She has passed a finger across my lips, unfastened
The topmost pearl-snap button on her ecru blouse
(The sound a flame makes touched to glass, the glass
Then touched to water), and guided my hand
Held trembling beneath the rustle of that enfolded cloth.
And in that still assembling hour, assembling through

That same stirred waterlight that it did then,
I have felt for the first time in my life, have felt
As something inside of me, as another body within
My own, her breathing deepen, and its guttering.
Things aren't always what they appear to be,
And neither, I suppose, are the things we feel.

But the truth is I was scared to think that dream
Might actually *be* a dream, or that, in turn,
It might prove not to be a dream at all, for it seemed
Blood-bidden what happens then, when she eases
My hand to a place I can only conceive of as
A vacancy, a chill alongside that pillowed hillock
She had moved it from. She draws it, you see, along
The raised abrasion of a surgical scar that cut
In a transverse angle from her rib cage to her shoulder.

And that, she whispers, is the reason she's come.
The reason she's left the party upstairs. The reason
She simply wants me now to look at her, wants me
Just to look and see the body her husband refuses
To see. But could that really have happened?
I wondered about it even then. And how
Could it possibly end in tears? The tears that all
Too readily come when she finally steps back
From my side, lets fall her blouse and underthings,
And stands there backlit by an aquarium glow
Her body inflected with a sorrow that lay
Well beyond the reach of my thirteen years.
And this is where I ask myself if all of this
Was only a fantasy, just another freak,
Enciphered scene unspooled from the bobbin

Of an adolescent's dream. Believing that,
My parents both earnestly stood their ground
The following fall, when her husband found her

Four months pregnant, sprawled out naked
On the bathroom floor beside an emptied bottle
Of Nembutal. I talked to people about it when
Things came to light. One caseworker in particular
Took the better part of an afternoon explaining
Why it was the letters this woman and I exchanged
Had nothing to do with love at all, not with
"Real" love anyway, but with something more—
How did he put it?—"unnatural," I think, though
Clearly he meant to say "perverse." I accepted that.
I saw the sense. But what I recall (and, admittedly,
It took me years to sort what's fact from fiction),

What I recall is that, as she stands there figured in
The pale aquarelles her ever-receding memory
Paint, I swim out toward her to be taken up by
The current of her inclining arms, to be folded back
Into another world where my own tears start,
Though what I wept for I can't say—*that* is what
I remember. That and the more unlikely fact
That all of this happened even as she was somehow
Muffling the sounds I could not keep down,
Easing me under and taking me in, taking me into
The mind's all suddenly silvered light, and inside that
To a welling in the blood, a fullness in the heart,
The secret, solitary, nowhere of a place wherein
One brief fluorescing stroke a shudder of grief
And arousal struck a lifelong, inwrought, echoing chord.

I can tell by the way you peer up over your glasses
That you're probably wondering why, in thirty-five years
Of marriage, I never told my wife about any of this.
But let me ask you something, now that our session
Has come to an end, now that I've chattered
On and on while you, as usual, say nothing.
Let me ask if you and the others
In your profession don't sometimes feel
Like the ones to whom it has devolved—
From God, no less—to serve as custodians
For our souls? The ones who keep from
Ravelling into oblivion that elaborate
Tapestry of self-delusions upon which
Our community now depends for moral
And spiritual guidance? No, I didn't think
You'd answer that. You're right not to, of course.

And so, the reason I haven't told my wife.
It's simple really. I just didn't want to hurt her.
I know you'll say my *not* telling her has hurt
Her more, but it seems to me, despite
That conventional wisdom, some truths
Can do more harm than good. Or maybe
I've only come to feel, as time has passed,
That we understand less than we pretend
About how to love, or why we should,
Or when it's right, or what we ought
To expect from it. And who's to say, given
The passionless affections, the pent-up malice

And forbearance with which most couples
Tend to treat each other for the better part
Of their married lives, who's to say that what
I had with that poor woman years ago
Wasn't actually love of a finer kind than I've
Known since, or am ever likely to know again?

A WRITER'S LIFE

for Charles Wright

My dearest Anne, How kind of you to take
The time to write and catch me up on things.
I miss so much our lunches after class, our talks,
Our walks along the river with your dogs.
And though I hold you dear in different ways,
You've become what I had hoped my daughter
Would become, were she alive today,
A companion with whom what narrow insight
Old-age affords might be exchanged
For that wide and mirrory outlook which now
Crowns your youth. But she is not alive,
Nor is my darling husband, and so it is
From time to time I think of you
As one of them. I hope you don't mind,
Or mind too much, for it's in that spirit
That I'll ask you, after I return, to tell me more
About your plans to take up writing
Now that you have finished school.
You are, you know, the brightest student
I have ever had, and I'd think you could do
Anything you want. Which makes me wonder
If you really want a life that's so . . . so what?
So *self-inflicted* as this one. Looking back
On fifty-odd years of it, I feel the kind of
Resigned acceptance one might feel for

A small deformity, or a slight impediment
Of speech which, however politely it's received,
Nonetheless makes one think there's less
To lose from saying nothing. Be that as it may,
It's certainly true that writing may provide
A "portal of escape" (the phrase, I believe,
is Ruskin's) into some less tiresome
version of ourselves.

                Speaking of which,
You'll be amused to learn the foundation
Has finally settled me into my very own
Ruined cottage, a stone, two-room
Fisherman's hut complete with a sway-backed
Roof that leaks, a rough wood floor,
And holes in the masonry large enough
To fire a sizeable cannonball through.
Creature comforts notwithstanding, I wake
Each morning perched atop a freshly wind-swept
Promontory three hundred feet above
The Irish Sea, a shelving aerie from which,
Whenever the weather breaks, I can see
All the way to the Isle of Man and across
To Galloway. On certain days it feels as if
I viewed the world from the highest terrace
Of human consciousness, a view
Like that which Wordsworth claimed,
Looking down on Chamouny from the Alps,
Made "rich amends" (though amends for what

I can't recall). Other days, I've found such
Pleasant consolations elude me altogether,
And this prospect settles upon my heart
A dull unshakeable sorrow, as though
I'd viewed the world from the raw perspective
Of the newly, prematurely dead.

                                                            Fortunately
The weather hardly ever breaks, for beyond
All that there's not much here but sheep
And us. Which prompts me to say, it didn't
Take long to fall back into the sheepish habits
Of our little flock. I write all day, then pass
The evenings in that guarded amity common,
I suppose, to writers' retreats all over the globe.
The dinners are served up "family style"—
Roasted chickens, legs of lamb, heaping bowls
Of boiled spuds laid out by six in the dining hall
Of a renovated fifteenth-century castle
We've nicknamed "Fortress Hunger."
The way we eat you'd think we'd actually
Spent our days plodding behind a horse
And plow; and afterwards, a turf-fire banked
Against the rising chill, we're invited to gather
In the sitting room for some pinochle
And inchoate chat.
                                    Lately, however, I find
I'm more inclined to watch, from an overstuffed
Armchair beside the fire, the *presqu'ile* city

Of an outgoing ferry crossing the horizon
Toward Scotland. It departs from Larne
Each night at nine, the final passage of the day,
I'm told, and it takes about three-quarters
Of an hour to slide across the windowpane
And disappear from sight. A great birthday cake
Of a ship with SEALINK blazoned in huge
Blue letters along its side, it moves so slowly
It's hard to tell it moves at all; and yet,
While it first sets off so brightly prinked
With running lights and cabin shine it casts
A green-gold shadow on the sea, it soon
Burns down to a smoldering glow, snuffed-out
Like a candle flame. One curious thing
About it is, no matter how hard I try,
No matter how fully I focus my attention,
I can never actually *see* it fade, I can never
Make out even one of those thousand
Fine gradations, even one of those
Incremental shifts by which it finally
Disappears.

       This will, I fear, sound strange
To you, but it's as though throughout
That brief excursion, that all-too-fleeting
Sleight of hand, I'd watched from afar
My own life pass across the windowpane:
How it set out glamored in the burnished hope
Of what they used to call "my gift,"

A sort of promissory note the Certitudes
Launched toward a future where,
At journey's end, it would be redeemed
In a light like that which falls across
The bees-waxed transoms of Vermeer.
But the journey, it happens, is not toward
Such fulfillments, nor have I ever (as I recall)
Been touched by any such light as that.
It's more as though, little by little,
In a slow declension imperceptible to sense,
The mind's eclipsed, the promise dims,
And the light goes out altogether.
And then one day you find yourself
Alone and a little embarrassed
That you've dared outlive your gift.

But knowing your tendency to give
Such things your full consideration,
I suspect you've already made your list,
The pros and cons of the writer's life,
And held them in the balance. And lest
My letter settles too easily on one side,
I'll confess that if I had it to do over,
If I knew in advance what I know now,
I'd make the same choices I did then,
Though I hope you'll simply entertain
The fact (or call it my strong impression)
That the supreme art is a happy life,
And a happy life anathema to art.

VI

A MOMENT

What I perceived is what I remember.

I didn't know her name.
She was thirteen or fourteen, I was twelve,
And we were somewhere in California.

Her family had rented a campsite
On the lake side of a trailer park,
Their sky blue octagonal tent
Opening outward on the water.

We'd spent all morning at the archery range,
And all morning our lead-
Tipped arrows traced
A liquid silence through the summer air,

Some errant, some true, some steered
As if by fortune
Toward the banked-up bales of hay.

When she slipped away in the afternoon
I watched her growing smaller
As she hurried down the trail.

On the lake, an older couple in a red canoe
Rowed out toward the opposite shore,
And with each inaudible
Oar-stroke the insect *chirr* grew louder.

And then, from a cloudless sky,
A light rain fell.

I heard it fall, passing across wide water
Onto land, the small drops
Dimpling the trail
With muffled, inexpressive thumps.

And without any thought of why or how,

I felt that moment take hold
In me, a moment
Without feeling or significance or form.

SENTIMENTAL EDUCATION

I. ROMEO & JULIET

With that same unsettling instinct for how
Human love can fall by chance to the borrowed
Grave of a coldwater flat, the forecast snows
Heaped up since dawn against our two small

Street-level windows, walling out the staticky,
Offstage noise of the early morning traffic,
The stink of trash and exhaust pipe fumes.
But when setting aside our breakfast trays

And drawing the goose-down coverlet off,
You climbed up over me, late for work,
And filled my mouth with a nut-brown,

Poppied aureole, I couldn't believe that either
Of us would ever die, or that, given the choice,
We wouldn't choose this and be buried alive.

II. SUMMER SOLSTICE, ISLANDMAGEE

With water hauled up from a rocked wellhead,
You'd fieldwash your breasts and underarms
In the sink where the dinner dishes steamed
Then follow the late-setting sun to bed.

Bathed in lantern-light, our gabled room
Had one small window through which, refreshed,
The sea wind amplified your nakedness
With the soft-bated breath of a Peeping Tom.

III. LAKE TAHOE, EARLY FALL

The flooding monochromes of sun and rain,
A high wind shear off the ridgeline, detached
Cloud banks rising up over the stunted pines,
Or settling around them in a smudgy crosshatch

Shadowing of spires, whole groves in succession
Dissolving into blear then emerging once more
Even clearer than they were, a rehabilitation
We warmed to later with our books and a fire

And felt glad to be out of it, holed up in a cabin
While we sorted things out, talking through
The brunt of it, and now and again, as if twinned
In spirit to the downfall beyond our window,

Conspiring to warrant the pains we'd take
To forswear those promises our natures break.

Like the two-story clapboard farmhouse
Which, in a tornado outside Moberly,
Missouri, lifted up off its stone foundation,
Rotated one hundred and eighty degrees,

Then settled back down without disturbing
The sleeping couple inside; or the nest
Of unbroken sparrow eggs found cradled
Inside the wheel well of an over-turned

Tractor trailer; or a child's blue-pedestaled
Lunar globe (first glimpsed by a guard
On cell block D) dropped upright into
The work yard of a maximum security prison;

So too does memory warm to recollect
The dazed amazement of a moment lifted
And settled back down amidst the rubble
Of what, twenty years later, we've come to call

Our "drinking days":

❖

      a motel in the compound
Of some border casino near Tahoe,
The two of us having lost the little we had
To lose, and for all of that I awakened

To the spill of water sounds, the dream shape
Of you standing naked, drying your hair
In a steamed-over, gradually clearing mirror,
The slow but certain coming-into-being

Of who you were, or of who, perhaps,
You'd hoped to be, the reverie of it
Playing across your face in shades I imagined,
First, of fear or loss, a feeling, in any case,

By which you'd summed up everything
We had handed down, open-eyed, to the iron
Uncertainties of happenstance. But no,
It seems I'd merely superimposed my own

Fears onto you and so invoked a fate
You'd prove the one reliable proof against,
For what happened next revised not only
What it was I thought I saw, but how

I've seen you ever since:

❖

                        you wrapped
A bath towel around your waist,
Knotted it at the side, and as if to set
Your own interior record straight,

Paused a moment to regard yourself
In the mind's eye of that mirror; and then,
Like a shipboard passenger gazing
Over the railing at some island slowly

Coming into view, there rose to the light-
Touched surface of your face a smile whose
Pure and unaffrighted calm composed
The world around you just as surely as

That half-turned house, those sparrow eggs,
That lunar globe inside the prison yard,
And the miracle of it (of you, my love)
Would never again be lost on me.

v. Illuminated Manuscript

Like motes embedded in the vitreous humor,
Those odd, unsorted cryptographs of memory
And blood underwrite our lives in texts, it seems,
We've somehow lost the sense to read; and yet,

Setting aside my book last night, I thought
For a moment I could just make out, beneath
The fluent features of your sleeping face,
The mute particulars of a dream begin,

Its self-reflecting secrets start to ramify
And clear: Your eyelids quickened, your brow
Assumed the furrowed look of someone
Reading on a garden bench (October

Sunlight fretting the page) a story more her
Than she now seems, a story undone
By the same pale photons and free-floating
Threads which, when the lamp's turned off,

Or the eyelid closes on a sun-touched page,
Resolve into our field of vision as a lost
Cuneiform of burnished signs whose meanings
We've somehow unknowingly become.

SMOKE TREE

Seeking out sun from beneath

A spreading sycamore, it fountains over
    Our front door in a long-limbed,
        Liquid, sideways arc, a kind of airily

Maintained *yogin*'s bend it gains

By virtue of a mystic struggle for the world
    Of light; and having moved there-
        By both heaven and earth, it fulfills in us

The idea of a life

Inclined to assume the burnished illogic
    Of what it believes (and how
        Else could we rise up into an element

So remote from us?) and the spirit in which
    That belief is held. Still, love,
        Lest we should take too seriously the soul's

Priority in such things,

It makes a game of us each spring when, leaving
    Home in the mornings, we're forced
        To stoop to hurry beneath its dipping limbs,

The same spare limbs which, pruned back

In October, somehow overnight have grown
	Dense with pale, exfoliate
		Blooms, their million rose-gray filaments tipped, each

	With a pinprick drop of dew:

Little planetaria turned inside out
	Or, touched by sun, a crystal
		Starburst fireworks show which even the most lack-

	Luster breeze, or squirrel's leap

From limb to limb, will shake down on us a sil-
	Very shower of light and rain,
		A chill exhilaration we quicken to

	With a goose-bumped, breathless, earth-

Bound thrill the flesh transfiguring figures through
	A language that imagines
		Our storied bodies come crisply into leaf.